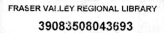

Tales of Famous Animals

Tales of Famous Animals

Peter and Connie Roop

Illustrations by Zachary Pullen

SCHOLASTIC REFERENCE
An imprint of
■SCHOLASTIC

The authors wish to thank the staff at the Cleveland Museum of Natural History for their invaluable assistance with Balto and the staff at the Rockport Public Library for their assistance with Andre.

Peter and Connie dedicate these tales to these tails:

Leah's Jocey

Bobby's Timmer

Heidi and Peter's Kuna

John and Marti's Troll

Jake and Laura's Tillie

Peter and Susie's Marcus

Martha and Joe's Abbie and Quincy

Meaghan's Pepper

D.R. and DeDe's Zeus

Ron and Harriet's Jazz

Karen and Jim's Schooner

Sue and Ed's Quimby

Ellen and Ray's Tully and Carley

Nona and Rick's Sally

Amy and Roger's Louie

Pat and Skip's Eli

Caleb's Kaiser

Faye's Sissy

Connie's Ming Toy

Peter's Butch

Library of Congress Cataloging-in-Publication Data Available

ISBN 978-0-545-43029-6

10 9 8 7 6 5 4 3 2 1   12 13 14 15 16

Printed in China   38

First printing, December 2012

Illustrations by Zachary Pullen created using oil on linen.

Text is set in Rosemary and Gf Index.

Book design by Chelsea C. Donaldson

Contents

Bucephalus
(Macedonia, modern-day Greece)

King Philip and his son Prince Alexander watched Bucephalus enter the courtyard. The untamed black horse reared on his hind legs. He struck out with his front legs. The grooms could barely hold on to Bucephalus's reins.

Bucephalus was the horse Alexander would ride from Macedonia to India as he conquered the world. Bucephalus the brave-hearted would carry Alexander the Great thousands of miles. He would ride fiercely into battle after battle with Alexander on his back.

Alexander was approximately twelve years old on the day he met Bucephalus in perhaps 336 BC. Later it would be said both boy and stallion were the same age. On this day, no one could control Bucephalus. His master wished to sell the powerful horse to King Philip of Macedonia, now the northern part of Greece. King Philip ordered that Bucephalus be taken away. He would not have a horse that no one could control. Alexander admired the strong-spirited horse.

Bucephalus means "Ox-head," and he was so named because his head was shaped like an ox's. Alexander told his father that it would be too bad to lose such an excellent horse simply because the groomsmen could not control him. King Philip ignored his son. Alexander repeated his concern for losing Bucephalus several times. Finally, King Philip suggested that maybe Alexander could manage Bucephalus better. Alexander rose to the challenge. He said, "I could manage this horse better than others do." King Philip asked Alexander what he would pay if he could not control the wild Bucephalus. "I will pay," answered Alexander, "the whole price of the horse." The king and his men burst out laughing. How could a boy as young as Alexander control such an unruly, gigantic horse? Where would he get the silver to pay for Bucephalus if he failed?

According to the Roman historian Plutarch, Alexander observed Bucephalus when he reared and snorted. Alexander saw that Bucephalus was afraid of his own shadow.

Each time Bucephalus faced his shadow, he thought he was being challenged by a huge black horse.

As any full-blooded stallion would do, Bucephalus fought his enemy. Alexander gently took the reins. He turned Bucephalus toward the sun so his shadow disappeared. Alexander talked to the mighty horse. He stroked his mane and rubbed his back. When Bucephalus had calmed down, Alexander leapt lightly onto his back. Bucephalus, sensing that Alexander was his partner, galloped off. King Philip and his men were amazed.

When Alexander and Bucephalus came back, the men cheered. King Philip wept with pride at what his brave son had accomplished. Plutarch writes that Philip said to Alexander, "O my son, look thee for a kingdom equal to and worthy of thyself, for Macedonia is too little for thee." King Philip was right. Alexander would one day conquer a kingdom that stretched from Greece to India. In his quest for greatness, Alexander would rule parts of modern Greece, Turkey, Syria, Israel, Lebanon, Egypt, Iraq, Iran, Afghanistan, Pakistan, and India.

For most of this amazing adventure, Alexander rode Bucephalus. They fought together, never losing a battle from Macedonia to India. Alexander trained Bucephalus to be a warhorse. He taught him how to attack and use his feet against an enemy. He trained Bucephalus to wear armor on his legs and his massive chest. In battle Bucephalus would wear a red harness and a red saddle cloth. Astride Bucephalus, sixteen-year-old Alexander first led troops against a rebellious tribe and defeated them. Alexander renamed his enemy's main town Alexandropolis. This was the first of many cities Alexander named in his own honor. One day, Bucephalus would be honored in the same way.

King Philip was murdered when Alexander was only twenty years old. Alexander was now the sole ruler of Macedonia and much of what is now Greece. But Alexander had a dream. He wanted to conquer the immensely wealthy Persian empire, ruled by Darius, which stretched from the Mediterranean Sea to the Indus River.

Alexander led his men into battle after battle. Alexander and Bucephalus would plunge into the enemy's army. Together, they led their men and horses to victory after victory. Once, an enemy captured Bucephalus from Alexander. Alexander threatened to destroy the region's inhabitants unless Bucephalus was returned. The unharmed horse was soon safely back with his mighty master. Twice, Alexander defeated Darius's army, but the first time, Darius escaped. Finally, the day came when Alexander and Darius would battle for the last time. Alexander, far from his home base in Macedonia, had fewer men than Darius but greater courage and leadership. In addition, Alexander rode mighty Bucephalus. Together, Bucephalus and Alexander led the charge, vastly outnumbered. Alexander won once more, but again Darius escaped. This time, however, Darius died while Alexander chased him. Persia and its immense wealth now belonged to Alexander the Great and his faithful men.

But Alexander had a new dream. He wanted to cross India and reach the far eastern sea.

Some of Alexander's men were restless. They had been away from friends and family for years. They had conquered Persia and been rewarded with their fair share of Persia's treasures. They wanted to return home.

By willpower and leadership, Alexander convinced his army to cross the Indus River and reach what is now Pakistan. However, Porus, an Indian rajah and leader, was equally determined to turn Alexander back. The two armies clashed on the banks of the Jhelum and Chenab rivers. Bucephalus, now old and battle scarred, charged against the enemy's huge war elephants, which towered like armored walls above him. The battle raged for days until Alexander realized that even he must retreat. Alexander's march eastward had finally been stopped. He would return west to enjoy the treasures of the lands he had conquered.

During this last battle, Bucephalus was wounded, and he died. Alexander, friend and master of the mighty Bucephalus for many years, buried his faithful companion. The grieving Alexander ordered that a city be built on the grave of Bucephalus. The city, in Pakistan, was named Bucephala in honor of the great horse that carried Alexander as he conquered the world.

MISSOURI
RIVER

Seaman
(Pittsburgh, Pennsylvania)

In 1803, President Thomas Jefferson sent Captain Meriwether Lewis on a mission. Captain Lewis, with his friend Lieutenant William Clark, was to try to find the Northwest Passage, a water route across North America to the Pacific Ocean. President Jefferson called this expedition the Corps of Discovery.

People had searched for this waterway to the west since Christopher Columbus's time. But no one had found it. President Jefferson was determined to see if the Northwest Passage really existed. If it did, then people and trade goods could cross America from sea to shining sea. President Jefferson selected Captain Lewis, a former soldier and his personal secretary, for this important mission. Captain Lewis chose Seaman to be his four-footed companion on this heroic adventure. History does not tell us exactly when Captain Lewis bought Seaman, his prized Newfoundland dog. We do know the big black dog was with Captain Lewis when he left Pittsburgh, Pennsylvania, on a new keelboat in August 1803. Captain Lewis and Seaman were beginning the most famous journey of discovery in America's history. They were going to cross the continent to the Pacific Ocean, about three thousand miles away. Why did Captain Lewis pick a Newfoundland dog to join him on his journey? Newfoundlands were popular. Both George Washington and Benjamin Franklin had owned Newfoundlands. These intelligent, faithful dogs are good workers. Newfoundlands also have strong, webbed feet and are outstanding swimmers.

Both Captain Lewis and Lieutenant Clark kept journals in which they recorded their many adventures. They also wrote down details about the weather, the Native Americans they met, the land, the water, the minerals, and the soil. In their journals, Seaman comes alive as one of the most important members of the Corps of Discovery. One day in September 1803, Captain Lewis saw many squirrels swimming across the Ohio River. At Lewis's command, Seaman eagerly leapt off the keelboat, swam to a squirrel, caught it, and brought it back to Lewis. This was the first time Seaman was mentioned in Captain Lewis's journal. Lieutenant Clark and dozens of men joined Captain Lewis before they headed downstream to where the Missouri and Mississippi rivers meet. Lewis wrote about Seaman again when a Native American wanted to buy the handsome dog. He offered three valuable beaver skins in exchange. Captain Lewis would not sell his beloved companion. It was

OREGON
COUNTRY

SPANISH
TERRITORY

UNITED
STATES

*Journey of
Lewis and Clark*

a good decision. He had paid $20—approximately half of his monthly pay—for Seaman. But over the next three years, Seaman proved again and again that he was indeed priceless.

On May 14, 1804, the Corps of Discovery began the long, hard journey up the Missouri River. The men worked their keelboat and pirogues (canoes) as they struggled upstream against the Missouri's mighty current. Each man ate nine pounds of meat every day to keep up his strength. The expedition's hunters shot deer, elk, antelope, and buffalo to feed the hungry men. Seaman hunted, too. He gathered geese, beavers, and deer shot by the hunters. Once, he even caught an antelope swimming in the river, killed it, and brought it back to shore! One day, Seaman captured a swimming beaver. Suddenly, the beaver slashed Seaman with its sharp teeth and sliced open an artery in one of Seaman's legs. Blood spurted from the wound! Captain Lewis carefully tended to Seaman's leg. That night, Lieutenant Clark wrote, "Capt. Lewis's dog was badly bitten by a wounded beaver and was near bleeding to death." The tough but gentle Seaman survived his injury and returned to his place as a valuable member of the expedition.

One night after the men had gone to sleep, a huge buffalo charged into camp. Seaman bravely chased it out of camp. Because of Seaman, the sleeping men were saved from being trampled by the buffalo's sharp hooves. Seaman's biggest job was warning the men about grizzly bears.

Seaman's keen sense of smell alerted him when a ferocious bear was near. His barking warned the men of the danger.

Captain Lewis wrote, "Our dog gives us timely notice of their [bears'] visits. He keeps constantly patrolling all night." On their long journey, Lewis and Clark met numerous Native Americans. Many were impressed by Seaman's faithfulness and intelligence. One day, three Native Americans stole Seaman. Captain Lewis sent armed soldiers to rescue his dog. Seeing the soldiers, the Native Americans released Seaman unharmed.

In November 1805, almost eighteen months after they began their journey, Lewis and Clark reached the Pacific Ocean. They were disappointed that they hadn't found the fabled Northwest Passage but excited that they had reached the Pacific.

Seaman had become the first American dog to cross the continent. Captain Lewis was so proud of Seaman that he named a Montana creek in his honor. Lieutenant Clark wrote the name Seaman's Creek on his map. Today, Seaman's Creek is called Monture Creek. History fails to tell us just what happened to Seaman. He disappears from Captain Lewis's journal in July 1806. Did Seaman fall behind when Lewis and his men were chased by Native Americans, and remain out west? Did Seaman stay with the expedition when it returned triumphantly to Saint Louis, Missouri, on September 23, 1806? We do know that brave, faithful Seaman stepped into history when Captain Meriwether Lewis decided he was the only dog for the Corps of Discovery.

Jumbo
(London, England)

Have you ever eaten jumbo shrimp? Or had a jumbo-sized drink?
Or flown in a jumbo jet?

How did Jumbo, the world's most famous elephant, give his name
to gigantic things?

Jumbo's tale begins in East Africa, where he was born in 1860. Jumbo was only a year old when he was captured and sent to faraway Europe.

Young Jumbo was a tiny elephant.

He was not expected to survive his months-long journey to Europe.

Jumbo, however, did survive. He walked hundreds of miles alongside dozens of other captured animals—ostriches, camels, antelopes, and giraffes. Jumbo rode on ships north along the coast of eastern Africa and then west across the Mediterranean Sea to Europe.

Europeans were familiar with elephants from Asia. But an African elephant, with its huge ears, was a marvel. When Jumbo stepped ashore in Italy in 1862, he was the first African elephant in Europe in two thousand years.

Jumbo went to a zoo in Paris, France. Jumbo stood only four feet tall. Zoo visitors were not impressed. When the Paris zoo bought two other African elephants, French officials sold Jumbo to the London Zoo.

Matthew Scott, a skilled animal caretaker at the London Zoo, became Jumbo's keeper and much-needed friend. The two met when Jumbo was five years old, weighed four hundred pounds, and measured five feet tall. Not much of a jumbo-sized elephant, especially for an African elephant, which can grow up to thirteen feet tall at the shoulders and weigh fourteen thousand pounds.

Jumbo had been mistreated in the Paris zoo. He had been kept in a small space. His feet were rotting. His hide was dotted with sores. His tail was falling off. His eyes were infected and he was almost blind. Scott was determined to save Jumbo's life. He wrote, "I undertook to be his doctor, his nurse, and general servant. I watched him night and day with all the care and affection of a mother." Scott fed Jumbo a special diet of straw, hay, boiled rice, bread, and biscuits. Slowly, Jumbo's health returned. And he grew. And grew.

Scott treated Jumbo with medicine, respect, and love. He had few human companions. Instead, he gave his heart to the animals in his care.

Abraham Bartlett, superintendent of the London Zoo, bought a female African elephant named Alice to keep Jumbo company. Jumbo and Alice became friends. Scott often took Jumbo down to the river Thames to bathe. Crowds gathered to watch Jumbo play in the river and spray them with water. Scott led Jumbo around the paths of the zoo. Excited visitors fed Jumbo treats. When the zoo's band played, Jumbo trumpeted along with the music. Sometimes Jumbo stole Scott's hat. Scott demanded his hat back. As the crowds laughed, Jumbo gently put Scott's hat back on his head. Jumbo gave rides to children for a penny. Gigantic Jumbo was called "the children's friend."

Crowds grew at the zoo.

By 1880, Jumbo stood eleven and a half feet tall and weighed fourteen thousand pounds. Jumbo had a jumbo-sized problem. He did not like to be kept inside at night. During the day, Jumbo was a gentle giant, but at night, he could be a terror.

He often attacked his building at night. He broke windows. He smashed doors. Superintendent Bartlett could not risk having Jumbo hurt someone, especially a child. The solution to Bartlett's problem arrived from the United States. Bartlett received a telegram from circus owners P. T. Barnum, James A. Bailey, and James L. Hutchinson, who ran the Greatest Show on Earth. The telegram asked, "What is the lowest price you can take for the large male African elephant?" Bartlett replied, "Will sell him for £2,000 [$10,000]." The British public was angry about Jumbo's sale. Parents complained. Children cried. Queen Victoria was said to have sent a telegram urging Jumbo's sale be stopped. A Jumbo Defence Fund was started, but a judge said Jumbo would have to go to the United States. Record numbers of visitors came to the zoo to see their beloved Jumbo before he was shipped across the Atlantic.

In March 1882, Jumbo entered the strong crate made to carry him to the United States. After sixteen years as a London Zoo star, Jumbo began another long journey. His friend Matthew Scott traveled with him to New York City. More than ten thousand people came to Madison Square Garden to see Jumbo's first performance. During his circus performances, he delighted the crowd by trumpeting with the show's band. Jumbo seemed to like the circus. His behavior improved. He didn't struggle to break free at night. Jumbo carried children on his back. Adoring crowds cheered and fed Jumbo oranges and buns. After a month, the circus traveled by railroad to Philadelphia, Washington DC, Cincinnati, Saint Louis, and Chicago.

Jumbo became a household word. People sold Jumbo pipes, Jumbo steam whistles, Jumbo statues made of glass, china, or rubber.

In 1883, Jumbo again thrilled crowds in New York and other cities. Barnum built the world's largest tent and filled it every night with twenty thousand circus fans. Millions of Americans enjoyed Jumbo's performances.

Sadly, a train engine accidentally hit Jumbo on September 15, 1885, in Saint Thomas, Canada. Jumbo died with his human best friend beside him. In 1985, a life-sized statue of Jumbo was erected near where he died.

The next time you say or hear the word *jumbo*, remember the African elephant that made such a jumbo-sized impact on so many lives.

Old Abe
(Eau Claire, Wisconsin)

Many soldiers had pets for mascots during the Civil War. One soldier had a dancing pet squirrel. Another soldier trained his raccoon to perform tricks. Jack, a dog, served in twenty battles and was wounded and captured by the enemy. The most famous Civil War mascot, however, was Old Abe, a majestic bald eagle.

In the summer of 1861, just as the Civil War was beginning, Chief Sky captured a baby eagle. Chief Sky, a Chippewa Native American, lived in western Wisconsin. He traded the young eagle to Mrs. Daniel McCann for a bushel of corn. Mrs. McCann and her family treated the eagle like a pet. The McCann children caught fish, mice, and rabbits to feed the hungry eagle. Mrs. McCann tied a blue ribbon around his neck. His new nest was a wooden barrel. Mr. McCann enjoyed playing his fiddle. The young eagle enjoyed the music. He hopped. He fluttered his wings. One day, the growing eagle escaped. When he was recaptured, the McCann family had a decision to make. They could not keep the fierce, strong eagle any longer. What could they do? Mr. McCann took the eagle to Eau Claire, Wisconsin. A band of soldiers had gathered there. The soldiers would fight for the Union army of the North against the Confederate army of the South. Mr. McCann sold the eagle to a man for $2.50. The man gave the eagle to the soldiers. Many of the soldiers admired President Abraham Lincoln. They also admired their new eagle mascot. President Lincoln was nicknamed "Old Abe," so the soldiers named their eagle Old Abe in honor of President Lincoln. The soldiers also named their own regiment the Eau Claire Eagles. The Eau Claire Eagles joined other soldiers in a big camp. The men marched with Old Abe. A band played "Yankee Doodle." Old Abe, excited by the music, grabbed the corner of an American flag. He flapped his wings and held out the flag. The crowd cheered.

The soldiers made a new perch for Old Abe that was shaped like a shield. It was painted with stripes. Old Abe had a wooden bar to stand on. A strong rope was fastened to him so he could not fly away. James McGinnis, a soldier from Eau Claire County, was given the job of caring for and carrying Old Abe.

The Eau Claire Eagles trained hard to become good soldiers. They marched. They practiced with their rifles. They learned to follow orders and work as a team. Finally, the Eagles were ready to go to war. Old Abe was ready, too. On October, 12, 1861, the Eau Claire Eagles and Old Abe left for Saint Louis, Missouri, ready for the front. The soldiers would camp near Saint Louis before going to fight in the South.

Old Abe's first battle was in Mississippi. The Union soldiers were attacked by Confederate troops. The battle was fought hard on both sides. Old Abe was sent to the rear for his protection. When the soldiers of Old Abe's company lay down so cannonballs would not hit them, Old Abe ducked, too. And when the men stood up to fight, Old Abe flew back on top of his perch. The Union troops were forced to retreat, including Old Abe's men. After the battle, General William Jackson Palmer praised the courage of the "regiment that bore the eagle." The Wisconsin soldiers were nicknamed the "Eagle Regiment," a name they carried with as much pride as they carried Old Abe. In another battle, a bullet cut Old Abe's leash. Old Abe, freed, flew screaming over the

Union line of soldiers while enemy bullets whistled through the air. David McLain, Old Abe's caretaker then, jumped up and chased Old Abe. Bullets riddled his shirt and pants, but he wasn't wounded.

Old Abe was shot at, too! He lost feathers from his tail and wings.

Old Abe, like all bald eagles, had feathers to spare. Bald eagles have seven thousand feathers to help them fly and keep warm. Finally, McLain gripped the loose end of Old Abe's leash. Then he grabbed Old Abe, tucked him under his arm, and ran to safety.

Stories spread about Old Abe's bravery under enemy gunfire. The Union soldiers were proud of their daring eagle. The Confederate soldiers tried to capture Old Abe. They aimed their rifles at him during battles. One soldier said that a Confederate general had offered a reward for Old Abe, "dead or alive."

Life in the army was not all battles for Old Abe. The soldiers spent a lot of time marching or in camp between fights. Old Abe sometimes caught fish, a bald eagle's favorite food, to eat. Old Abe played tricks of his own. He ran off with bullets that rolled onto the ground. He overturned water buckets. He ripped clothing with his sharp beak. He stole chickens the soldiers had saved for their own dinners. But even when the soldiers got angry at Old Abe, they continued to love and protect their mascot.

In 1864, after more than thirty-seven battles and skirmishes, Old Abe returned to Wisconsin. By now, Old Abe had matured and had a bald eagle's characteristic white head and white tail feathers.

Old Abe retired from the army along with many of his companions in the Eau Claire Eagles. The soldiers voted to give Old Abe to the state of Wisconsin. Governor James T. Lewis said that Wisconsin would care for Old Abe "as long as he lived." Old

Abe's fame had spread. People across America wanted to see Old Abe, the Civil War eagle.

When the Civil War ended in 1865, Old Abe began his new life. He made special appearances to raise money for wounded soldiers and their families. He visited fairs. He marched in parades with veteran soldiers. One Chicago newspaper said, "Old Abe . . . was the chief lion [featured guest] of the day, sitting upon his perch with immense dignity, flapping his wings and screaming."

In 1876, when the United States celebrated the one hundredth anniversary of the signing of the Declaration of Independence in Philadelphia, Old Abe was a star of the event. He met President Ulysses S. Grant, the general who led the Union army to victory in the Civil War. He had his picture taken, which was a rare treat at the time. Old Abe even autographed his pictures by piercing them with his beak! Old Abe continued to live at home in a special cage in Wisconsin. But sadly, one day in 1881, Old Abe died from breathing smoke when his building caught on fire.

Old Abe's memory is kept alive in books, pictures, and statues. The most famous statue of Old Abe is perched on top of the Wisconsin Monument at Vicksburg, Mississippi. Old Abe's men helped General Grant capture Vicksburg in July 1863. And Old Abe still flies into battle. The famous "Screaming Eagles," the 101st Airborne Division, are named in Old Abe's honor. These brave men and women proudly wear an eagle on a shield on their uniforms.

Punxsutawney Phil
(Punxsutawney, Pennsylvania)

Groundhog Day is celebrated every February 2, when Punxsutawney Phil and other groundhogs across the United States make their annual predictions about the end of winter. Each year, weather watchers eagerly await Phil's and his fellow groundhogs' forecasts.

Tradition says that if Phil sees his shadow, there will be forty-two more days of winter. If Phil fails to see his shadow, spring will soon be coming. Phil's forecast is enjoyed by millions of people around the country. Punxsutawney Phil is the most famous weather-predicting groundhog in the United States. But Phil is not the only groundhog predicting winter's end. From New York to Washington State, many states and cities have groundhogs forecasting the weather on February 2. Dave delivers his forecast in Dunkirk, New York. Jimmy makes his predictions from Sun Prairie, Wisconsin. West Orange, New Jersey, promotes Essex Ed. Raleigh, North Carolina, relies on Sir Walter Wally. New York City depends upon Staten Island's Chuck, and Lilburn, Georgia, trusts General Beauregard Lee to predict winter's length. The list of groundhogs able to predict the weather goes on and on.

The tradition of predicting the weather on February 2 comes from Europe. There, farmers used hedgehogs to forecast the length of winter. These burrowing, spiky, round animals hibernate in the winter, just like North American groundhogs.

If a hedgehog saw its shadow and scurried back into its burrow, Europeans believed winter would last six more weeks. No shadow meant spring was near.

Why February 2?

February 2 is about halfway between the winter solstice, the shortest day of the year, and the spring equinox, a day of equal light and dark.

The ancient Celts believed the beginning of February was the start of spring. They celebrated with a festival of lights. Christians call this day Candlemas, a festival of candles. They say:

"If Candlemas Day be sunny and bright,
winter will have another flight;
if Candlemas Day be cloudy with rain,
Winter is gone and will not come again."

German immigrants who moved to Punxsutawney, Pennsylvania, in the nineteenth century continued to celebrate Candlemas. At first, they hunted the hibernating groundhogs. But by 1887, the German residents were using groundhogs to predict the weather just as they had used hedgehogs back in Germany.

In the same year, some Punxsutawney men formed the "Inner Circle" of the Punxsutawney Groundhog Club. The Inner Circle now handles and protects Phil and other groundhogs that have their own special "burrow" at Punxsutawney Public Library. The usually sleeping groundhogs can be seen inside the library's children's section as well as twenty-four hours a day from the outside window. The men of the Inner Circle wear tall stovepipe hats like the ones Abraham Lincoln wore. The president of the Inner Circle claims to be able to converse with

Phil in "Groundhogese." This is why only he can understand Phil's predictions.

Like all groundhogs, Phil whistles when in danger. A nickname for groundhogs is in fact "whistle pig." Groundhogs are also called woodchucks. Have you heard the tongue twister: "How much wood could a woodchuck chuck if a woodchuck could chuck wood?" No one knows the answer to how much wood Phil could chuck, but we *do* know he would throw the wood backward! Phil's muscles are designed to pull back, not to push forward. Phil hibernates each winter. If Phil were in the wild, he would go on a special diet to get fat all through the summer. Wild groundhogs eat about one third of their body weight each day, about four pounds of food. They like to eat dandelions, daisies, lettuce, spinach, berries, pumpkins, peas, squash, cucumbers, green beans, and zucchini. In fall, Phil snuggles up in his burrow to sleep until early spring, almost half a year later.

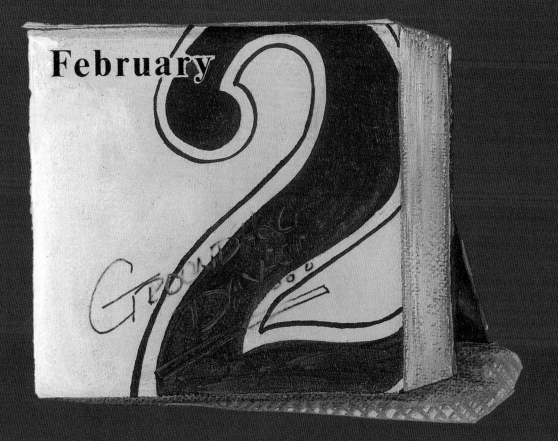

Of course, each February 2, Punxsutawney Phil is woken up from his long winter's nap by the Inner Circle to make his forecast.

Most groundhogs live about seven years, but Punxsutawney citizens claim Phil is over one hundred years old. Every summer, Phil sips magical "groundhog punch" made by the Inner Circle. One sip of this secret recipe guarantees Phil seven more years of life, according to the Punxsutawney Groundhog Club.

Folks in Punxsutawney, Pennsylvania, where Phil lives, say his predictions are 100 percent accurate. However, Phil has been correct only 39 percent of the time, according to meteorologists. What do you predict? Will Phil, Dave, Jimmy, Essex Ed, Chuck, or General Beauregard Lee see his shadow next February 2? Will there be forty-two more days of winter, or will spring come early? Watch for Phil and his friends to make their forecasts on February 2. Then see how much longer winter really lasts!

Pelorus Jack
(Pelorus Sound, New Zealand)

In 1888, a ship steamed toward French Pass, a dangerous strait in New Zealand. Water can speed through the narrow gap at nine miles an hour. That is three times faster than an adult walks.

The Maori, the native people of New Zealand, call these raging seas at French Pass Te-Aumiti the "Swirling Current." One lone lighthouse warned ships of the hazards. If a ship's captain made a mistake, he would wreck his ship on the rocky shores. Six miles from French Pass, just off Pelorus Sound, sailors aboard one ship were astonished to see a large dolphin suddenly appear. The dolphin slipped through the ocean, riding the waves made by the front of the ship. To the sailors, it seemed that the dolphin was guiding them safely to French Pass.

Just before French Pass, the dolphin disappeared. The sailors wondered at the dolphin's strange behavior. They were even more puzzled when, on their return journey, the same dolphin swam with them until they safely reached Pelorus Sound again. From 1888 until 1912, the dolphin, Pelorus Jack, guided dozens of different ships to safety. As each ship steamed along, Pelorus Jack rode its bow waves. Pelorus Jack's fame spread throughout New Zealand and around the world. Newspaper reporters told tales of Pelorus Jack. Magazine writers wrote stories about him. Photographers took his picture. Famous writers, like Rudyard Kipling and Mark Twain, wrote and talked about Pelorus Jack. Pelorus Jack poems were written. Tourists sent postcards of the famous dolphin to friends and family around the world. Pelorus Jack became so popular that he had his own chocolate bar!

A song was even written about popular Pelorus Jack.
"Everyone cheered whenever he appeared,
 Pelorus, Pelorus, good Pelorus Jack."
Bill Morrison, who ran a hotel near French Pass, painted a huge white sign on a big, flat rock announcing that Pelorus Jack could be seen from his porch. Over the years, scientists studied the unusual behavior of this remarkable dolphin. They said that Pelorus Jack was a Risso's dolphin. Risso's dolphins, one of the largest kinds of dolphins, live in warm waters around the globe. They live offshore and are usually found in deep waters. The scientists were puzzled, therefore, that Pelorus Jack lived close to shore. Scientists were also surprised that Pelorus Jack always swam alone, not in a pod like other Risso's dolphins did. And although his name was Pelorus Jack, scientists said that the amazing dolphin may have been a female. Was Pelorus Jack really Pelorus Jill? Tourists took trips just to see Pelorus Jack.

These excited visitors crowded their ships' sides, hoping to see the unique dolphin leap, dive, and splash in front of them.

"Here he comes!" someone would shout and point. Everyone would watch as the playful dolphin raced toward the ship, sped ahead, and rode the waves splashing off the ship's bow. Mrs. C. Blair, a passenger, said, "We all thronged to the bow of the ship to see a large silvery-white fish plunging through the waves towards us."

Pelorus Jack usually swam with each ship for about twenty minutes or up to six miles. Sometimes he even rubbed his back against the moving ship. The famous dolphin also made nighttime appearances. When he knew a ship was coming, Pelorus Jack would rush to it like a bolt of underwater lightning. Fred Barltrop, a sailor, wrote, "If you can visualize a mass of phosphorescent fire [about] fourteen feet in length travelling through the water with the greatest of ease, then suddenly leaping into the air, the spray and dripping water from him giving one the impression of innumerable fine flashes of electricity, you will get some idea of what Jack looked like." Pelorus Jack's phosphorescence was like the light a lightning bug makes at night. His phosphorescent fire was made by tiny ocean animals that glowed when he swam through them. When two ships came at the same time, Pelorus Jack swam with the fastest ship.

"The faster the boat, the greater the fun," one boy said.

George Webber was thirteen years old when he first saw Pelorus Jack. Each week, Webber and his father collected mail from ships steaming through French Pass. Their mail boat was fourteen feet long. When Pelorus Jack swam beside the boat, it was easy to measure him. Webber said, "He was not as long as the boat, and my father and I estimated he was between eleven and twelve feet long." Sometimes, Pelorus Jack was too friendly for Webber and his dad. He would bump their boat from beneath. Webber had to push Pelorus Jack away with an oar so he would not capsize their boat. Not everyone liked Pelorus Jack. One story tells of Pelorus Jack swimming to an approaching ship. Suddenly, someone fired a rifle at him. Unhurt, Pelorus Jack swam safely away. Whenever this ship came to French Pass again, Pelorus Jack refused to swim with it.

Pelorus Jack became so popular that the government of New Zealand passed a law in 1904 protecting him and other Risso's dolphins swimming in the area. This was the first time any government had ever protected dolphins. Many Maori were not surprised by Pelorus Jack's behavior. These native New Zealanders had many legends about dolphins guiding and rescuing people. According to the Maori, New Zealand's North Island is shaped like a dolphin with its tail in the air and its mouth pointing to New Zealand's South Island. Another Maori story tells how a helpful spirit in the form of a dolphin named Tuhirangi guided canoes safely through the same waters that Pelorus Jack did.

Then, one day in 1912, a ship passed the mouth of Pelorus Sound, but Pelorus Jack failed to appear. Had Pelorus Jack been killed? People worried. More ships steamed into French Pass, but still no Pelorus Jack. Webber, who had watched Pelorus Jack for twenty-four years, wrote, "It is my impression that he was an old fish and died from natural causes." In fact, Risso's dolphins do live to be about twenty-five years old in the wild. The *Marlborough Express*, the local newspaper, wrote, "'Jack' has been rightly termed one of the wonders of the world."

Today, Pelorus Jack is the symbol of New Zealand's Interislander ferries. These ferries still pass through the same dangerous waters where Pelorus Jack once guided ships.

The Roosevelts'
White House Pets
(Washington DC)

Presidents and their families have had many pets in the White House. But no first family had the zoo President Theodore Roosevelt and his energetic family had.

During their time as first family from 1901 to 1909, the Roosevelts had at least forty romping, galloping, slithering, swimming, and flying pets.

Many Roosevelt pets lived in the White House in Washington DC. Other favorite pets lived at Sagamore Hill, the Roosevelts' home on Long Island, New York.

President Roosevelt had six children: Alice, Archie, Kermit, Ethel, Theodore Jr., and Quentin. President Roosevelt loved his children dearly and enjoyed their company. They played games, read out loud together, hiked, had pillow fights, and roughhoused. One friend wrote, "The President runs at large and plays like a boy let loose for the holidays." When he was away from his family, Roosevelt wrote long letters, calling his children his "Bunnies" and telling them about his adventures. Once, as part of the US Navy in Cuba, Roosevelt wrote Ethel, "Here there are lots of funny little lizards that run about in the dusty roads very fast, and then stand still with their heads up." In another letter, he described a pig named Maude and a litter of newly born puppies.

Over the years, before the Roosevelt family lived in the White House, they had many different pets. When the Roosevelts moved into the White House in 1901, they brought many of their pets with them. They had a beautiful macaw named Eli. There was also Jonathan, a rat "of a most friendly and affectionate nature, who crawls all over everyone." There was a flying squirrel, two kangaroo rats, and the hens, Baron Speckle and Fierce. Peter the rabbit and a small bear named Jonathan Edwards joined the romping Roosevelt menagerie. Tom Quartz, a kitten, was a Roosevelt family favorite. President Roosevelt said, "Tom Quartz is certainly the cunningest kitten I have ever seen." Tom was always playing tricks on Jack, the Roosevelts' terrier dog. Tom would sneak up on Jack and jump on him. He would hide and then leap on poor Jack.

One night, Tom Quartz raced after Joseph Gurney Cannon, the Speaker of the US House of Representatives—a very important man! He grabbed Cannon's leg with his sharp claws, then jumped off, full speed ahead. Cannon, a frequent guest at the White House, was not the least surprised by Tom's sudden attack, as he knew about the kitten's wild behavior.

Once, a little girl gave President Roosevelt a small badger. President Roosevelt named him Josiah, or Josh for short. He said, "He is very cunning and I hold him in my arms and pet him. I hope he will grow up friendly." When Josh arrived at the White House in 1903, the president said, "Josiah, the young badger, is hailed with the wildest enthusiasm by the children." On one trip, the president caught a horned toad he named Bill the Lizard. He couldn't wait to get home and share his new treasure with his family.

When the family was away, President Roosevelt himself had to care for two of Ethel's guinea pigs because she would not trust them with anyone except her father.

The Roosevelts especially enjoyed dogs. They had many different dogs, from Rollo, a huge Saint Bernard, to Manchu, a small Pekingese. Sailor Boy, a Chesapeake retriever, would swim after their boat if the Roosevelts left him behind. Skip, President Roosevelt's favorite, was indeed the "top dog" at the White House and enjoyed many privileges. Skip, a black-and-tan terrier, went hunting with the president. He raced down the halls of the White House. He even rode on the back of Archie Roosevelt's pony, Algonquin. When Skip died, President Roosevelt sadly said he had had "a happy little life."

Not all the Roosevelts' pets lived at the White House. Many lived at the Roosevelts' home on Long Island. People enjoyed giving the Roosevelts animals as presents, but there was no place for bears, a zebra, a hyena, and a lion in Washington DC, so they were given to a zoo.

Alice, the oldest Roosevelt child, had a green pet snake she named Emily Spinach. Alice loved to surprise people. She would wrap Emily Spinach around her neck or hide the snake in her purse to scare people. Quentin also liked snakes. One time, he was loaned three snakes from a pet store. Quentin went to the Oval Office to show his new treasures to his father. The president was having an important meeting, but his guests

smiled at the excited boy and his snakes. President Roosevelt's guests thought the snakes were toys. They were quite surprised to find out Quentin's snakes were real! President Roosevelt was "dee-lighted" at this trick, but the snakes were returned to the store.

Algonquin, a black-and-white Shetland pony, was another favorite White House pet. On the frequent horse rides the family took, Archie always rode Algonquin. He even gave Algonquin Christmas presents. One time, when Archie was sick, he worried about Algonquin. He missed the pony. Quentin wanted to cheer up Archie, so he decided to secretly bring Algonquin up to Archie's bedroom on the third floor. Quentin knew that Algonquin would be seen climbing the stairs, so he took Algonquin up in the White House elevator! Archie was thrilled to see Algonquin. Algonquin did not want to get out of the elevator because he was enjoying his own image in the elevator mirror.

"I don't think that any family has ever enjoyed the White House more than we have," President Roosevelt said. The many Roosevelt pets seemed to enjoy their time in the White House, too.

Oh Joy! Wonderful

20-Inch $1.75 Teddy Bear

This pleasant looking bear is made of good quality cinnamon color plush. Fully jointed, glass eyes. We offer this serviceable toy at a very low price. Shipping weight, 2½ pounds.

48D3201—Price only $1.75

39c

59c 10-Inch Teddy Bear

We have endeavored to give the little tots the best bear we could procure at a low price. Made of good quality cinnamon color plush. Has natural looking eyes. Head, arms and legs are jointed. Ship

59

The First Teddy Bear
(Brooklyn, New York)

Do you have a teddy bear? Millions of children (and adults) around the world have one or more of these famous stuffed bears. Did you know that the teddy bear was named after President Theodore Roosevelt, in 1903?

Energetic Theodore Roosevelt loved to be outdoors. He enjoyed acquiring special animals for his children. He spent time outside riding horses, hiking, collecting, and learning about the environment. One of Roosevelt's favorite activities was hunting. He had hunted in western states and eastern states. But he had never had the opportunity to hunt in the South. In November 1902, when Roosevelt was president, he took time from his busy schedule to go bear hunting in the thick forests of Mississippi. President Roosevelt, several friends, and a flock of newspaper reporters rode the train to the small town of Smedes, Mississippi. There, Holt Collier, an experienced guide and hunter, joined the group. The men headed off into the forest. Roosevelt was eager to hunt, but he also wanted to enjoy the huge cypress and cottonwood trees. He wanted to ride through the miles of swamps and see the plentiful wildlife. Collier led the way through the tangled forest. He knew the woods well. Collier, an African American, had been born a slave in 1846. He had been a skilled hunter since age ten, when he killed his first bear. Collier had also been a Confederate soldier, a Texas cowboy, and an animal tracker.

Collier and Roosevelt enjoyed each other's company. Both men had lots of energy. They liked the hardships of living outdoors while hunting. And they were both accomplished storytellers, spinning yarns of their adventures around their campfire in the evening. Collier even showed Roosevelt his scar from the bear he had killed with a knife when he was just a boy. Collier was known as the best bear tracker in Mississippi, maybe in all of the United States. Collier knew how bears behaved. He knew where they slept at night and where they found their favorite foods, such as berries, nuts, melons, persimmons, and honey. With Collier in charge, President Roosevelt would most certainly get a black bear and have fun while doing it.

One reporter wrote, "The President is enjoying his outing very much. He has not had three days of such complete freedom and rest since he entered the White House."

On the morning of November 14, Collier's dogs smelled a bear. They cornered it. The bear fought desperately to save its life against Collier's raging dogs. Collier, not wanting to shoot at the bear and accidentally hit one of his dogs, smacked the bear so hard with his rifle that the barrel bent! Finally, the bear was subdued—but not killed. Collier, who had been ordered to let President Roosevelt shoot the first bear they found, tied the injured bear to a tree. When President Roosevelt, an honorable sportsman, saw the exhausted bear tied to a tree, he refused to shoot it. Tweed Roosevelt, President Roosevelt's great-grandson, wrote, "Any good hunter realized that to have shot that particular Mississippi bear would have been cowardice. As a true hunter-conservationist, T.R. [Teddy Roosevelt] would never have considered engaging in such a sordid act."

The story of President Roosevelt's sparing the bear made newspaper headlines. Then, on November 17, 1902, a cartoon by Clifford Berryman, often called "The Passing Show," appeared in the *Washington Post*. Berryman had drawn President Roosevelt's refusal to shoot a small bear being held by a man. Before long, the cartoon was enjoyed by millions of Americans, in newspapers throughout the country.

Rose and Morris Michtom in Brooklyn, New York, saw the cartoon. The Michtoms sold candy, stationery, and handmade toys at their small shop. Rose made two toy bears to show her approval of President Roosevelt and his compassion for the bear. She made her bears out of plush material, stuffed them, and gave them round, black button eyes. The Michtoms put one of their stuffed bears in their shop window. They called it Teddy's Bear, in the president's honor. Customers bought the two bears, and the Michtoms made more. These Teddy's Bears sold quickly, too.

The Michtoms thought that it would be a good idea to have Roosevelt's permission to call their bears Teddy's Bears. They wrote a letter to President Roosevelt in February 1903, asking if he would mind if they called their bears Teddy's Bears, after him. Roosevelt apparently wrote back to the Michtoms, but that letter has been lost. In the letter, Roosevelt is said to have written,

"I don't think my name will mean much to the bear business, but you're welcome to use it."

The Michtoms sold their Teddy's Bears for $1.50 each. Their bears and others like them became some of the favorite toys of children in the United States and Europe. By 1907, more than a million teddy bears had been sold. The Michtoms' Teddy's Bears were so popular that the Michtoms formed the Ideal Novelty and Toy Company. Other teddy bear manufacturers claimed that their teddy bears were the real thing, but President Roosevelt gave credit to Berryman and his hunting cartoon for starting the craze. In fact, Berryman always included a small bear whenever he drew a cartoon with President Roosevelt in it.

When William "Billy" Howard Taft became president in 1909, one company designed a new animal toy to honor him. The company created Billy Possum, a pink-eyed, grinning opossum. The company slogan said, "Good-Bye Teddy Bear, Hello Billy Possum." Instead, it was "Good-bye, Billy Possum." The ratlike toy was a sales disaster.

Today, boys and girls, men and women around the world have teddy bears. The bears lie on beds, sit on desks, are cuddled and hugged, given as gifts, shared in hospitals, used by emergency workers to give comfort to children, and even have their own Teddy Bear Society of America club.

Today, one of the Michtoms' original 1903 Teddy's Bears is on display at the Smithsonian National Museum of American History in Washington DC. But even though the beloved teddy bears remain so popular, President Teddy Roosevelt did not like the name. He wrote, "No one of my family, for instance, has ever used it [Teddy], and if it is used by anyone it is a sure sign he does not know me." But thanks to President Roosevelt's unwanted nickname and his sportsmanship with a bear, we have our beloved "Teddy's" bears.

Mrs. Chippy
(Antarctica)

In 1913, Sir Ernest Shackleton, a British explorer, was looking for men to join him on an expedition to Antarctica. Shackleton had been to Antarctica twice before. Once, he had even come within ninety-seven miles of the South Pole.

Roald Amundsen of Norway, however, had reached the South Pole on December 14, 1911. His expedition won the race to be first to the South Pole. Since Amundsen had already reached the South Pole, Shackleton was determined to be the first to cross the continent of Antarctica. Shackleton was looking for twenty-seven brave men to join his Imperial Trans-Antarctic Expedition. Shackleton advertised in the British newspapers.

Five thousand men and three women applied. Shackleton carefully selected twenty-seven men to join him. One was Harry McNeish. McNeish, fondly called Chips, was the ship's carpenter. McNeish brought along Mrs. Chippy, his tiger-striped cat. There are many stories about why. One story says that McNeish would miss Mrs. Chippy too much, so he brought his beloved cat on board. Another story says that Mrs. Chippy had curled up in McNeish's toolbox, so he took the cat along.

But no matter how Mrs. Chippy came to be aboard Shackleton's ship, *Endurance*, the cat was welcome.

Mrs. Chippy proved to be intelligent, friendly, and entertaining. Mrs. Chippy was also good at catching mice and rats, rodents that could have destroyed the expedition's precious supplies. Shackleton, his twenty-seven men, and Mrs. Chippy sailed from England on August 1, 1914. No one knew that this was to be a voyage of no return for the sturdy *Endurance*.

While crossing the Atlantic Ocean to South America, it was discovered that Mrs. Chippy was not a female cat but a male!

But Mrs. Chippy remained Mrs. Chippy.

In October 1914, the *Endurance* landed at Buenos Aires, Argentina. Little did Shackleton realize that Perce Blackborow, a young sailor, had hidden himself aboard the *Endurance*. Blackborow was discovered after the *Endurance* left port, but it was too late to take him back. Shackleton liked the young stowaway and signed him on to the crew. Blackborow became a valuable member of the crew. He was also one of Mrs. Chippy's best friends. Sixty-nine dogs had joined the expedition at Buenos Aires. These dogs, some part wolf and part husky and part other large breeds, were brought along to haul the heavy sledges of supplies across Antarctica. The half-wild dogs were kept in cages on deck.

Mrs. Chippy roamed the *Endurance* from stem to stern. He hunted mice and rats. He kept Blackborow company in the galley (ship's kitchen). He played games with the men.

One of Mrs. Chippy's favorite pastimes was to annoy the dogs. Mrs. Chippy moved quickly across the deck by walking on top of the dog cages. He would jump onto a cage and then stalk down the deck, keeping just out of the reach of the snarling dogs that would have eaten him if they had the chance. Mrs. Chippy kept himself clean by washing his paws and licking his fur.

The *Endurance* sailed south toward Antarctica. One night in, Mrs. Chippy accidentally fell overboard. The officer on watch, Lt. Hudson, heard Mrs. Chippy scream, turned the ship around, and picked him up. Mrs. Chippy surely used up one of his nine lives swimming in the freezing water that night.

The *Endurance* reached the Weddell Sea, off Antarctica, in December 1914. Soon, the hardy *Endurance* was sailing among towering icebergs. She pushed her way through huge floes of jumbled ice. And every day, the weather turned colder. The men enjoyed the birds soaring overhead. They watched seals swimming near their ship. They marveled at spouting whales and diving penguins. The *Endurance* steamed on even as the ice got thicker. Then, on January 18, 1915, the ice surrounded the ship. She could not move forward or backward. The *Endurance* was trapped in the ice!

For the next ten months, the ice held the *Endurance*. The expedition made the ship their camp. They were warm and safe in the tough ship. The dogs were moved into "dogloos," small igloos made of blocks of snow, on the thick ice. The men played soccer and hockey on the ice to keep in shape. They held dog races and acted in plays for entertainment during the long dark polar day and night. Mrs. Chippy continued prowling the ship, catching mice, chasing chess pieces, and purring in the sailors' laps.

But the ice was crushing the *Endurance*. The ship's timbers creaked, groaned, then cracked. The men wondered how long before they would have to leave the *Endurance* and move onto the ice. The end came on October 27, 1915. That day, Shackleton ordered the *Endurance* be abandoned. The men, the dogs, and

Mrs. Chippy would have to survive on the ice. The men gathered all the supplies they could reach in the ship. Then, on November 21, 1915, the ice released the *Endurance* from its grip. The men sadly watched their hardy vessel sink. Shackleton decided to travel over the ice to land. But the nearest land was hundreds of miles away. Shackleton told his men they could only bring two pounds of their own belongings. The rest of the room on the sledges would be for food and supplies. Unfortunately, there was no food or room for Mrs. Chippy and three newborn sled-dog pups to continue with the expedition.

Shackleton had a very difficult decision to make. If he left Mrs. Chippy behind, she would starve to death. If she came along, the dogs would kill her. Reluctantly, it was decided that Mrs. Chippy and the pups must be put down. Two more years passed before Shackleton and his men returned to England. They faced many more hardships, but not a single one of the men died on the expedition. Mrs. Chippy was not forgotten. Harry "Chips" McNeish remembered his faithful companion until he died in 1930. He was buried in Wellington, New Zealand. In 2004, a life-sized bronze statue of Mrs. Chippy was placed on McNeish's grave. Together, these two brave explorers are honored and remembered for their contributions to the exploration of Antarctica.

Balto
(Anchorage, Alaska)

"Nome calling . . . Nome calling . . . We have an outbreak of diphtheria . . . No serum . . . Urgently need help . . . Nome calling . . . Nome calling . . .

On January 20, 1925, this telegram went out over the Alaskan wires. Diphtheria, a deadly disease, had struck Nome, Alaska. Children were dying. The people of Nome desperately needed a lifesaving serum to protect them from diphtheria. This medicine was in Anchorage, Alaska. But how could it be carried from Anchorage to Nome, more than a thousand miles away? No train, plane, boat, or truck was able to make the journey. In the winter, only a sled-dog path called the Iditarod Trail linked Anchorage and Nome. Dogsleds took almost a month to deliver mail using this trail. Could dogsleds follow the Iditarod mail trail to deliver the lifesaving medicine? Yes!

A relay of dog teams was quickly organized. Expert mushers (the men who drive dogsleds) and their strong dogs pitted their lives against the blinding snow and dangerous trail. Would these courageous sled dogs and the mushers arrive in time to save the people of Nome? The serum from Anchorage arrived by train to Nenana. The first musher, "Wild Bill" Shannon, dashed off with his team from Nenana on January 27, 1925. Shannon carried twenty pounds of precious serum lashed onto his sled. The thermometer read forty degrees below zero. The temperature dropped to minus fifty degrees as Shannon and his determined dogs raced toward Tolovana, the end of their relay run. They traveled fifty-two miles in the frigid cold and blasting snow. The race for life, a 647-mile race against time, began.

The second leg of the relay began when Edgar Kulland's team ran the serum to Dan Green at Manley Hot Springs. The relay continued day and night. Different mushers continued to carry the lifesaving medicine toward Nome.

They traveled blind when the swirling snow caused whiteouts. Mushers' hands froze in the icy temperatures. The valuable serum froze in its warm coverings. Would it still be good against diphtheria? Despite the blasting wind and brutal cold, the mushers kept going. Two dogs froze to death. Their musher hitched himself into the lead dog position to pull his team to the relay point. Famous musher Leonhard Seppala and his lead dog, Togo, joined the relay. On January 31, this brave team safely crossed the Norton Sound in a storm. Three hours later, gale force winds broke up the Norton Sound ice. The Seppala and Togo team had barely avoided disaster.

The howling wind and blinding snow continued. Seppala passed the serum to Charlie Olson, and Olson to Gunnar Kaasen. Kaasen chose Balto as his lead dog. Balto was an intelligent black Siberian husky. Huskies have thick fur and powerful, compact bodies designed for running fast. Their keen sense of smell, up to one thousand times a human's, allows them to follow snow- and ice-covered trails. Balto's big chest helped him be an extremely strong dog. A serious storm raged. The dogs yelped, yipped, and jumped. They were eager to run. "Mush!" Kaasen commanded on February 1, 1925. The team had thirty-four miles to go before they got to the next relay station and dogsled team. Determined, Balto plunged headlong into the dark, raging storm, leading his ten dog teammates. The dogs raced with their ears pinned back. The curved, flexible wood sled glided over the rough trail. Snowdrifts blocked the trail. Balto tried to blast through. Some dogs panicked as they sunk up to their bellies or necks in snow. But Balto remained calm. Kaasen dug the dogs out of the deep snow. Balto led the team around the snowdrifts and found his way back to the trail.

Nome waited as time ticked by. Balto continued to guide the sled to the Topkok river. Suddenly, he stopped. "Mush!" Kaasen demanded. Balto refused to move. "Mush!" Kaasen repeated. Balto continued to disobey his master. Kaasen walked to the head of the sled.

Balto was standing in shallow water. The ice had cracked! Balto had saved the team and its valuable cargo from falling into the Arctic river water.

Balto faced the danger of frozen feet. Kaasen dried his paws with powdery snow before the team pushed on.

Ready to race again, Kaasen looked down into the sled. The serum was gone! In the dark and with his eyes stinging from arrows of ice, Kaasen dug bare handed in the snow, searching for the medicine. At last, he found the precious serum!

After midnight, Balto guided the sled into Point Safety, the last relay station with a new musher and dogs. Kaasen was looking forward to resting, getting warm, and feeding his dogs. But the station was dark. The weather was too bad. The musher had gone to bed and was not ready to sled the medicine to Nome. Valuable time would be lost to wake up the musher and harness his team of dogs.

Kaasen decided Balto and his team were strong enough to run the remaining twenty-one miles to Nome. Point Safety to Nome was the last leg of the journey from Nenana.

On February 2, 1925, at five thirty in the morning, Balto safely guided Kaasen and the dog team into Nome. Exhausted and nearly frozen, they delivered the lifesaving medicine. The dogsled teams of Alaska made the journey of 674 miles in just five and a half days, a world record. News of this courageous and dangerous race for life made headlines all across the United States. Balto was famous!

A Hollywood movie producer brought Kaasen, Balto, and the rest of the sled dogs to Los Angeles. The famous sled-dog team toured the United States. The same year, 1925, a statue of Balto was placed in Central Park in New York City to celebrate the historic race of life to Nome.

Balto lived the rest of his life at the Brookside Zoo in Cleveland, Ohio. He died on March 14, 1933. He was fourteen years old. The Iditarod, the world-famous dogsled race from Anchorage to Nome, takes place every March. This challenging dogsled race celebrates the pioneer spirit of brave sled dogs like Balto. Balto remains a symbol of courage, intelligence, and sacrifice.

Lonesome George
(Galápagos Islands, Ecuador)

Why is George lonesome? George, a giant Galápagos tortoise, is lonesome because he is the last tortoise of his kind.

"We're 99.9 percent sure he is the last individual of his species," explains David Wiedenfeld at the Charles Darwin Research Station, in the Galápagos Islands, Ecuador. Hundreds of thousands of giant tortoises lived on the Galápagos Islands four hundred years ago. But from thousands to hundreds, George's kind of giant tortoise is now one. Once George dies, there will be no more giant tortoises like him. They will be extinct, gone forever.

Giant tortoises are one of the most amazing animals living in the Galápagos Islands. They are indeed gigantic. Some tortoises weigh up to five hundred fifty pounds and measure five feet long. George weighs about two hundred pounds and looks like a large boulder when he is inside his forty-inch shell.

Galápagos giant tortoises are land animals. George looks like a prehistoric creature when he extends his wrinkly, brown, three-foot-long neck to slowly chomp on cactus. Galápagos tortoises live longer than any other vertebrate, some more than 150 years. No one really knows how old George is, but a good guess is about seventy-five years old. Charles Darwin, an English scientist, visited the Galápagos in 1835 and was enthralled by George's relatives. "I frequently got on their backs, and then giving a few raps on the hinder part of their shells, they would rise up and walk away." Darwin observed that tortoises "walked at a rate of 60 yards in 10 minutes . . . at this pace, the animal would go four miles in the day." He noted that when they drink, "they bury their heads to above their eyes in the mud & water & swallow about 10 mouthfulls [sic] in a minute."

Galápagos means "tortoises" in Spanish. George lives on one of the "tortoise" islands, called Pinta Island. It's near the equator in the Pacific Ocean, about six hundred miles west of Ecuador. Herman Melville, author of *Moby Dick*, described George's tiny northern island in the nineteenth century as "so solitary, remote, and blank, it looks like No-Man's Land." Fifteen types of giant tortoises were discovered on thirteen major islands in the Galápagos archipelago. Darwin came to believe different tortoise shapes resulted from each island's unique habitat.

George is one of the eleven kinds of Galápagos tortoises that still survive. But once George dies, there will be only ten types of Galápagos tortoises left on Earth. George will join the four other types of giant Galápagos tortoises that have already become extinct since humans first visited the Galápagos in 1535. These tortoises will never lumber along dry, dusty paths to cool pools to drink. What happened to all the tortoises like George?

Pirates and whalers were the first to discover the benefits of giant tortoises. Galápagos tortoises have good

Galápagos Islands

67

fat reserves. They can survive a year without food and water by living off their stored fat. When turned upside down, they pull themselves inside their hard shells. Sailors stacked the tortoises upside down on the decks of their ships. Many hungry sailors probably ate George's relatives on their long sailing voyages.

In 1813, US captain David M. Porter recorded in his journal that his men collected more than fourteen tons of giant Galápagos tortoises in four days to eat as fresh meat on their voyage. Only three of these captured tortoises were male. The rest were female. Unfortunately, sailors preferred the smaller and lighter females because they were easier to load onto their ships. David Farragut, as a twelve-year-old American midshipman, witnessed English sailors on the whaling ship *Georgiana* throwing several hundred Galápagos tortoises overboard as they cleared the decks for battle. Farragut wrote in his diary that "they floated as light as corks, stretching their long necks as high as possible, for fear of drowning. They were the first we had ever seen, and excited much curiosity as we pushed them aside." After winning the battle, the crew of his ship, the *Essex*, later brought about fifty of these tortoises on board and ate them throughout their voyage.

Dozens of ships visited Pinta Island to take giant tortoises for food. Eating females meant fewer eggs.

Fewer eggs meant fewer tortoises on Pinta Island. Fortunately, George's mother survived to lay eggs.

Animals and plants people introduced to the Galápagos Islands created another problem for Galápagos tortoises. On Pinta, goats brought to the island enjoyed eating the same bushes and plants as the tortoises. With less food, the tortoises on Pinta Island struggled to survive. Collectors made George more lonesome, too. When George hatched in the early 1900s, scientists and individuals were racing around the Galápagos, collecting each kind of tortoise for zoos, museums, and private collections. Before the discovery of George, the last reported sighting of a giant tortoise on Pinta Island was in 1906.

George surprised everyone.

Joseph and Maria Vagvolgyi discovered George on December 1, 1971. Joseph was studying snails. He recalls, "The tortoise was walking slowly when we first encountered him, but withdrew into his shell with a loud hiss as we moved closer to take his picture. He soon relaxed and resumed his walk."

George is now the most famous reptile in the world.

Today, George lives in the Charles Darwin Research Station in the Galápagos. Scientists have tried to make George less lonesome. They scoured Pinta Island for another tortoise. A $10,000 reward is offered for a female tortoise from Pinta Island. Scientists tried to make George a dad by breeding his with closely related tortoise relatives. No Father's Day for George yet.

Each year, thousands of tourists visit Lonesome George. A sign near George's pen at the research station reminds them, "Whatever happens to this single animal, let him always remind us that the fate of all living things on Earth is in human hands." Hopefully, Lonesome George is not the last of his kind.

Seabiscuit
(Kentucky)

The starting bell rang. Thirteen horses surged out of the gate. "And they're off!" called the racetrack announcer. The world's race with the biggest prize was on!

The horses thundered down the track. "Here comes Seabiscuit!" someone shouted. "Here comes the Biscuit! Here comes the Biscuit!" roared thousands of fans at California's Santa Anita racetrack. Seabiscuit's hooves pounded the ground. Red Pollard, Biscuit's jockey, urged the short brown horse to put his big heart into the race. Seabiscuit sprinted to the finish line to win. Seabiscuit had lost this race twice. But today, March 2, 1940, was Seabiscuit's day. The crowd roared for their hero, Seabiscuit, America's wonder horse.

When Seabiscuit was born in Kentucky, on May 23, 1933, he did not act like a champion racehorse. He was small. His legs were thin. He wobbled like a duck when he ran. Seabiscuit tried to bite or kick anyone who came near him. Seabiscuit, however, had the blood of racing champions. Man o' War, his grandfather, was one of the United States' best thoroughbred racing horses. Hard Tack, his father, was a champion, too. Seabiscuit raced eighteen times before he won.

But in his first win, Seabiscuit tied the racetrack record. In his next race, he beat the record.

In 1935, when Seabiscuit was just two years old, he raced thirty-five times. Few colts ran that many races in one year. Seabiscuit had the talent to win, but he was lazy.

Seabiscuit's owners decided to sell him. But no one wanted the bad-mannered colt. One day, Tom Smith, a talented horse trainer, watched Seabiscuit race. "Rear view, front view, all around—he kind of struck my fancy," Smith said. After the race, he nodded at Seabiscuit. "Darned if the little rascal didn't nod back," he said. He whispered to Seabiscuit, "I'll see you again." Smith spoke to Charles Howard, his boss, and said, "Get me that horse. He has real stuff in him. I can improve him. I'm positive." Howard and his wife, Marcela, bought Seabiscuit for $8,000 in August 1936. Smith was the skilled, caring trainer Seabiscuit needed to make him a winner. Seabiscuit now had owners who saw his racing potential. But what jockey could win while riding cantankerous Seabiscuit?

Small, fiery-tempered Red Pollard proved to be that jockey. In 1936, Pollard, like millions of Americans, was down on his luck. He had few riding jobs. The country was in the middle of the Great Depression. Millions of people had lost their jobs. Many had lost their homes. Americans needed a hero to take their minds off the Depression's tough times. Bad-tempered, lazy Seabiscuit would become that national hero.

Smith made Seabiscuit feel at home in his stable. A wall of his stall was knocked down to give him more room. Smith thought Seabiscuit needed animal companions to calm him down, so he put a goat in Seabiscuit's stall. Seabiscuit tossed the goat out. Smith put a pony named Pumpkin in with Seabiscuit. Seabiscuit and Pumpkin quickly became friends. A dog named Pocatell and a monkey named Jo Jo also joined him. Smith worked hard to earn Seabiscuit's trust. He talked to him. He let him sleep late. He fed him a special diet. He rubbed Seabiscuit's knobby legs. Smith said, "We had to rebuild him, both mentally and physically, but you don't have to rebuild the heart when it's already there, big as all outdoors." Seabiscuit became better behaved. And with Pollard aboard, Seabiscuit ran faster and faster.

Howard and Smith decided it was time for Seabiscuit to enter a big race, California's Santa Anita Handicap. The winner won $100,000! The race was on March 6, 1937. The race bell rang and the

SPORTS | S | SPORTS
HORSE of the YEAR
SPORTS | G

horses took off. Seabiscuit was in fourth place, then third, then second, then first place. But another horse, Rosemont, caught up with Seabiscuit. Seabiscuit and Rosemont raced across the finish line. Rosemont won by a nose! The Seabiscuit team was not discouraged. They believed Seabiscuit could be a champion. They were right. Seabiscuit won races and broke records. The knobby-kneed horse was becoming an American favorite.

Seabiscuit, however, was not the United States' best horse. War Admiral, Seabiscuit's "uncle," won all his races in 1937 and was named Horse of the Year. Nineteen thirty-eight was Seabiscuit's year. He lost another close race at Santa Anita, but then he hit his stride. He won race after race. Fans across the country kept up with Seabiscuit's career. Seabiscuit came in first in newspaper reports in 1938, surpassing both President Franklin Roosevelt and German leader Adolf Hitler. Seabiscuit was Horse of the Year.

Then tragedy struck. On June 23, 1938, Seabiscuit's favorite rider, Red Pollard, was seriously injured while riding another horse. A different jockey rode Seabiscuit in the "race of the century," on November 1, 1938. War Admiral and Seabiscuit shot out of the gates when the starting bell rang. Seabiscuit quickly took the lead. Suddenly, War Admiral raced up to him. Would this be another heartbreaking loss for Seabiscuit? No! Seabiscuit pulled away from War Admiral and thundered to the finish line. Seabiscuit was now the champion of champions!

In a race in early 1939, Seabiscuit badly hurt his left leg during a race. People thought neither he nor Pollard would ever race again. But Seabiscuit showed his true spirit. Smith slowly got Seabiscuit's injured leg healthy. Pollard shared Seabiscuit's same determination and got his own leg healthy, too. By 1940, Seabiscuit and Red Pollard were ready to race again. The Seabiscuit team believed they could win the Santa Anita Handicap, the same race they had lost twice before. And they did! Pollard said, "The greatest ride I ever got from the greatest horse that ever lived."

After this race, Seabiscuit retired to the Howards' ranch, where he lived until his death on May 17, 1947. In 1941, a life-sized statue of Seabiscuit was unveiled at the Santa Anita racetrack. The inscription of his statue reads, "Biscuit's courage, honesty, and physical prowess definitely place him among the thoroughbred immortals of turf history. He had intelligence and understanding almost spiritual in quality."

Long after Seabiscuit's heroic last race, people still remember the determination and courage of America's wonder horse.

FIRE DANGER

EXTREME

TODAY!

PREVENT FOR

Smokey Bear
(Capitan Mountains, New Mexico)

"Remember—Only You Can Prevent Wildfires!"—Smokey Bear, United States Department of Agriculture

Smokey Bear, famous for fire prevention, was born on August 9, 1944. Well, not really born, but created by illustrator Albert Staehle. Staehle was hired to create a mascot for the United States Forest Service. The United States needed a special animal mascot to spread the word about preventing forest fires. In 1943, Walt Disney gave permission for the government to use an image of the deer Bambi to help in this fire prevention effort. Bambi, who escaped a terrible forest fire, seemed to be the perfect animal to lead the fight against forest fires. But Disney allowed Bambi to be used for only just one year.

Another animal was needed to spread the word about protecting our forests. When Bambi could no longer be used, the government searched for an animal to replace the popular deer.

On August 9, 1944, Staehle drew the first picture of Smokey Bear pouring water on a campfire. This became Smokey Bear's official birthday.

The first Smokey Bear said, "Care Will Prevent 9 out of 10 Forest Fires!" This early warning would be changed in 1947 to the famous line "Remember—Only You Can Prevent Forest Fires!"

Over the years, the Smokey Bear cartoon character was given a ranger hat with his name on it. He began wearing blue jeans with a Smokey belt buckle. Smokey also carried a shovel to put out fires.

In May 1950, a terrible forest fire began burning in the Capitan Mountains in New Mexico. Most likely, the fire was started accidentally. Strong winds quickly spread the fire through the dry forests. Firefighters were called to the rescue. Many of these brave men were trained firefighters. Others were local ranchers and cowboys. Some were Native Americans. Several were soldiers from Texas.

At times, the fire seemed to be under control. But sparks jumped over the firefighters and ignited new areas. The fire raced up mountains and down into valleys. Trees exploded into flame. Animals tried to escape, but many died. One brave group of men was trapped by the fire. The fire burned behind them, leapt over them, and surrounded them. Their quick-thinking leader, Speed Simmons, kept the men from running. He knew they could not outrace the fire. Simmons led his men to a rocky landslide. He told them to lie facedown. Burning embers set their clothes on fire, but their companions quickly put out the flames. The men narrowly escaped death.

When the fire had passed, Simmons and his men saw a blackened landscape. The fire had destroyed almost every living thing. Surprisingly, the men heard a whimper like a baby crying. They saw a baby bear cub clinging to a charred tree. The bear cub had survived the fire! Simmons rescued the bear. Its feet were burned and bleeding. Its bottom was blistered. The baby bear was starving without its mother.

The men took the frightened bear to their camp. They named him Hotfoot Teddy. Hotfoot Teddy was renamed Smokey Bear. Before long, Smokey Bear became the most famous animal in the United States.

The men fed Smokey Bear candy bars and milk. But this food made him sick.

Ray L. Fell, a New Mexico Department of Game and Fish pilot, came to the rescue. He put the five-pound bear into a shoe box and flew him to Dr. T. J. Smith, a veterinarian in Santa Fe, New Mexico. Dr. Smith bandaged Smokey's feet and took care of his many burns. But Smokey still wouldn't eat food that was good for him. How could Smokey's life be saved? wondered Dr. Smith. Fell and his daughter, seven-year-old Judy, came to the rescue. When Judy learned that Smokey would not eat, she said, "I know Mother can make him eat, whether he wants to or not."

So they took Smokey home. Ruth Fell fed Smokey a mixture of cereal, honey, and milk. Before long, Smokey's wounds had healed. And he was growing like a bear cub should. Smokey became well known locally. His picture was in the newspaper. Children came to visit him. He had his picture taken licking Judy's face. People around the United States saw this picture and were happy that Smokey has been saved. Lyle Watts, chief forester of the forest service, learned about Smokey, the real bear. He thought Smokey would be a wonderful symbol of the need for people to prevent forest fires. He suggested that Smokey come to live in the National Zoo in Washington DC. Smokey was flown to Washington DC in a small plane with a picture of Smokey Bear painted on the side. A huge crowd met Smokey when his plane landed. Smokey moved into his new home at the zoo. He quickly became one of the zoo's most popular attractions. Smokey was on TV. He was on the radio. His picture was on posters all across the United States telling people to be careful with fire. The song "Smokey the Bear" was written about him:

"Smokey the Bear, Smokey the Bear.
Prowlin' and a-sniffin' the air.
He can find a fire before it starts to flame.
That's why they call him Smokey,
that was how he got his name."

"He is a live Smokey helping carry on the work of the poster Smokey," wrote the forest service. Smokey became so famous that a secretary was hired to answer the thousands of letters he received. He even had his own zip code, 20252!

Smokey Bear lived until he was twenty-six years old. He was buried near his childhood forest in New Mexico. A big stone marks his grave. The sign on Smokey's grave says he had become "the living symbol of wildfire prevention and wildlife conservation." Watts said, "If Smokey could talk, I'm sure he would tell us plenty about the need for protecting our forests and all the wild creatures in them." Through his famous image, Smokey Bear indeed "spoke" to Americans about preventing wildfires.

Andre
(Rockport, Maine)

Imagine swimming in the ocean, sliding down a snowy hill, splashing in the bathtub, and riding in the car with a harbor seal pup! For twenty-five years, Andre, a harbor seal, did all these things and more with Harry Goodridge and his family in Rockport, Maine.

Goodridge was a skin diver. He swam underwater with a mask and flippers to fix boat moorings and do other underwater jobs. He wanted an animal companion to swim with him. Goodridge loved animals. He was especially curious about harbor seals and wondered if a harbor seal might be a good companion. He decided to find out.

Goodridge captured Andre on May 16, 1961. Andre was swimming off Robinson's Rock, a ledge where harbor seals rest and give birth to their babies. Instead of swimming away, Andre looked Goodridge in the eye. Goodridge assumed this nineteen-pound, two-day-old seal was an orphan because no mother seal was around.

Goodridge brought Andre home to his wife and five children. Andre's sleek, tear-shaped body fit into his "playpen," a bathtub in the basement. Goodridge took Andre in his car to swim in the ocean. At first, Andre did not like getting into the cold ocean water. Until a harbor seal pup gets fat, it prefers to live on land. Fat keeps the seals warm and helps them float. Mother harbor seals often have to force their pups into the icy ocean water by splashing or pushing them. Goodridge did the same with Andre. Goodridge frequently swam with Andre. As Goodridge had hoped, Andre was an excellent companion when Goodridge worked as a skin diver. Andre helped him retrieve objects deep underwater. If Andre swam away, he would soon return to check on Goodridge by smashing his whiskered face against his face mask. Andre enjoyed giving his an underwater ride; Goodridge would hitch a ride by hanging on to Andre's tail.

Goodridge quickly learned that Andre was very smart. He taught Andre tricks based upon actions he had observed in harbor seals. He asked Andre to roll over. Andre rolled over and swallowed his fish reward. Goodridge told Andre to clap his flippers. When Andre clapped his flippers, Goodridge eagerly flipped the fish reward into his mouth. The fish reward taught Andre he had done the correct trick.

Before long, Andre's dinnertime was filled with fun: jumping through hoops, shooting baskets, and shaking hands. People gathered to watch Andre show off. Andre liked having an audience as he performed for his meal of fish. Andre was friendly to fishermen. He rolled over by their boats to get his belly rubbed by their oars. But Andre got in trouble with fishermen, too. He crawled into their boats to rest or sleep.

Andre had grown so fat that he was difficult to push off the fishermen's boats.

Andre now spent almost all his time swimming in and around Rockport Harbor. But sometimes, Andre would disappear for days at a time. Goodridge always wondered if Andre would return.

As their first winter with Andre approached, the Goodridge family wondered what would happen to him. Would he leave when the harbor froze? If he did leave, would he ever return? If he stayed, would there be enough fish in the harbor for him to hunt? They knew most wild harbor seals followed fish farther away from shore in the winter. The Goodridges let Andre decide whether he would stay in Rockport Harbor for the winter or return to the wild. But they froze fish in case Andre stayed.

In November and December, Andre kept a hole open in the ice near the wharf. He popped his big, round head up through the thin layer of ice at the same time each afternoon to eat the fish Goodridge brought him.

Then, one stormy day in late December, thick ice covered Andre's hole, and Andre disappeared.

Goodridge told his family that Andre had left. No one knew what had happened to him.

In February, Goodridge read about a seal named Josephine. Josephine was in Marblehead, Massachusetts, more than 150 miles south of Rockport. She was friendly to fishermen and loved to soak up sunshine onshore. Josephine enjoyed an audience and did tricks for fish. Goodridge guessed Josephine was probably Andre. Goodridge asked his relative near Marblehead to identify Josephine as Andre. But Josephine disappeared before Goodridge's relative visited Marblehead. Several weeks passed. Then Goodridge received a phone call. A friend had spotted Andre on a beach in Rockland, not far from Rockport.

Goodridge dashed to the Rockland beach. It was a good thing he had come. Andre was hurt. He had cuts and bruises. One flipper was torn. He had infected sores on his belly. Andre's injuries may have been caused by fighting with another male harbor seal. Goodridge called Dr. McDonald, a local veterinarian, who gave Andre strong antibiotics. Happily, Andre recovered.

Rockport Harbor was Andre's summer home for the next twenty-five years. For his second summer, Goodridge built a pen for Andre to stay in each night. Each morning, Goodridge let Andre out. Andre lived as a playful pet. He learned more than fifty commands from Goodridge. He jumped through rings, retrieved toys, and quickly flapped out a piece of fiery newspaper with his flipper.

Thousands of people came to see Andre. "Pose for the camera, Andre," Goodridge directed. Curving like a rocking horse, Andre arched his huge, 240-pound, five-foot-long body and looked at the crowd with his whiskered face and round, brown eyes.

Rockport's manager named Andre the Honorary Harbormaster. Books were written about Andre. Maine's governor visited him. Andre was famous! In 1994, his story was told in a movie. In 1978, Andre unveiled a life-sized statue of himself. He pulled the cloth off the statue at its dedication ceremony. Andre's smooth gray marble statue still overlooks Rockport Harbor.

Later in life, Andre entertained visitors at the New England Aquarium in Boston, Massachusetts, or at Mystic Aquarium in Connecticut during the winter. Each spring, Andre was taken to Marblehead, Massachusetts. There, he was set free.

In 1985, Andre made his last journey from Massachusetts to Maine. He was twenty-four years old and nearly blind. He swam back to Rockport using his keen sense of smell and sensitive whiskers.

Andre died in July 1986. He was twenty-five, an old age for a harbor seal. Capture of a marine mammal like Andre is against the law today. But thanks to Andre and Harry Goodridge, we know harbor seals are curious, capable, and loyal animals.

Rockport, Maine

Marblehead, Massachusetts

Koko
(San Francisco, California)

"Fine animal gorilla," Koko signed to her friend and teacher Penny Patterson. Patterson answered with a huge hug for her friend and student. Together, Koko the gorilla and Patterson the human have taught people around the world about what it is like to be a gorilla. Patterson called their work together Koko's Project.

With Patterson's time, love, patience, and instruction, Koko became the first gorilla to learn a human language. With Koko's intelligence, skill, and patience, Patterson became the first human to learn what is like to be a gorilla. Francine "Penny" Patterson began working with Koko in 1972. Koko was only a few months old when she first met Patterson. After learning how Washoe, a chimpanzee, had learned to use her hands to sign language, Patterson thought she could teach a gorilla to communicate, too. Patterson decided to try to teach a young gorilla American Sign Language, or for short, ASL. Hundreds of thousands of deaf Americans use ASL, the fourth most common language in the United States. "When I began teaching Koko American Sign Language nine years ago," Patterson wrote in 1981, "I had no idea how far she would progress with it. There was little reason for me to assume that a gorilla could learn to use language to rhyme, lie, joke, express her emotions, or describe her world." Now, after forty years of working with Patterson, Koko knows over two thousand signs. She regularly uses more than five hundred of them to answer questions, ask for things, tease, show how she feels, and tell about what it is like to be a gorilla.

Koko was born on July 4, 1971, in the San Francisco Zoo. People were asked to name the baby gorilla. The winning name was Hanabi-Ko, which means "Fireworks Child" in Japanese, appropriate because Hanabi-Ko was born on the Fourth of July. Soon, the baby gorilla was nicknamed Koko. Patterson wanted to earn Koko's trust, so she carried baby Koko on her back around the zoo. When Koko felt more comfortable, Patterson began teaching the young gorilla the signs for *drink*, *food*, and *more*. Patterson signed the word to Koko and then shaped Koko's hand into the same sign. Each time Koko was given food or a drink, Patterson and her helpers repeated the signs for *drink*, *food*, *more*. But Koko did not use the signs without human help. After a month of working with Koko, Patterson was cutting some fruit, when Koko suddenly signed "food." Patterson said, "I couldn't believe my eyes. I wanted to jump for joy." Koko was so happy that Patterson was so happy that Koko put a bucket on her head and ran around her room, being silly. Koko quickly learned more words. When Koko was two years old, she put single words together to make requests. When she was thirsty, Koko signed, "Pour that hurry drink hurry." At her third birthday party on July 4, 1974, Koko signed, "More eat," after eating her whole birthday cake!

But life at the zoo was becoming more difficult for Patterson and Koko. Koko's room was too noisy, and there were too many distractions. Patterson moved Koko to her own special trailer

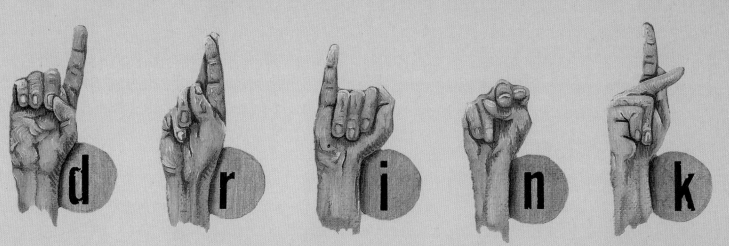

at Stanford University, not far from San Francisco. Patterson hoped that Koko could learn better in her new home. She did. At first, Koko did not like her new home. She signed, "Go home." Koko whimpered her gorilla crying noise, "whoo-whoo," at night. Patterson spent every night with Koko until she felt comfortable.

By age five, Koko could sign two hundred words.

Part of Patterson's work is to study Koko's behavior. Patterson recorded Koko's sounds. Dr. Ron Cohn, who had been with the Koko Project since its beginning days, videotaped and photographed Koko so her signs and behaviors could be studied later. Cohn's pictures of Koko were in magazines. Koko was on television. Koko even took her own picture, which was on the front cover of *National Geographic* magazine. Koko was becoming the most famous gorilla in the world.

Sometimes, Koko was naughty. She broke things. When Koko was naughty, she was punished by being put into a corner. When Koko felt better, she signed to Patterson, "Sorry. Need hug." And Koko got her hug. Patterson knew Koko needed a friend. After a long search, Patterson was able to bring Michael, a young male gorilla, to be Koko's new friend. Before long, Koko and Michael were playing chase together, enjoying hide-and-seek, and tickling each other, all in the way gorillas play. Michael, like Koko, learned sign language. "Tickle, please," Koko would sign to Michael, and a rough, wild game of tickling, chasing, and wrestling would begin.

Three Little Kittens is one of Koko's favorite books. Patterson would read it to her and ask Koko questions. Patterson decided to see if Koko wanted a kitten for a friend, too. Koko did. She gently played with her new furry friend. She picked up the kitten. She gave her kitten a rhyming name, All Ball. Koko's friendship with All Ball became a book and a film named *Koko's Kitten*.

Unfortunately, All Ball died one day. Patterson told Koko what had happened. Koko signed, "Cry, sad, frown," to show her feelings. Patterson got Koko a new yellow kitten, which Koko named Lipstick. In 1979, Patterson, Koko, and Michael moved to a different place in California. This ranch gave them room to roam without meeting too many people. Koko and Michael could also enjoy more time outside, climbing trees, wrestling, and playing chase. Koko usually has a very busy day. She eats. She learns her lessons. She has recess roughhousing time with Michael. She naps. She snacks. She goes for car rides. She uses her computer. She watches television. She meets famous scientists like Jane Goodall. She greets reporters and writers. At the end of her busy day, Koko gets ready for bed. Gorillas in the wild sleep in nests. Koko makes her nest out of an old tire and some blankets. After a good night's sleep, Koko is ready for another day.

In 2011, Koko celebrated her fortieth birthday, in her current home in the California Bay Area. Patterson and the group she founded, called the Gorilla Foundation, plan to move to Hawaii. Koko's new home on a tropical island will be much like the home her wild gorilla relatives enjoy in Africa. Unfortunately, Michael has died in the meantime. Together, Koko and Patterson have taught the world that gorillas can communicate with humans. Now Koko and Patterson are working hard to save endangered gorillas and to make sure that gorillas and humans can share the earth forever in the future. Koko is indeed a "fine animal gorilla."

Ling-Ling & Hsing-Hsing

(Washington DC)

On April 16, 1972, two large green crates arrived in the United States. The crates had been flown in secrecy—thousands of miles from China. Inside the special packages were two unique gifts to the American people from the Chinese.

Labels on each crate read in English and Chinese, "Giant Panda presented from . . . the People's Republic of China." Ling-Ling, which means "Cute Little Girl" in Chinese, was in one crate. Hsing-Hsing, or "Bright Star," a young male panda, was in the other. Together, these two giant pandas would become the most famous in the world.

China had sent the pandas to the United States as a special gift. A few months earlier, President Richard M. Nixon had become the first United States president to ever visit China. For many years, the United States and China had not been friendly to each other. President Nixon's visit and his wonderful welcome in China began a new era of courtesy between the two nations. To honor the occasion, China wanted to give the American people a special gift. What better present than two rare giant pandas that live in the wild only in China! The Americans gave the Chinese a gift, too—two furry musk oxen, Arctic animals the Chinese wished to have for the Beijing Zoo.

The two pandas were taken to their new home at the National Zoo in Washington DC. Although they had traveled in the same plane, neither panda had met the other. At the zoo, Ling-Ling had her own cage, and Hsing-Hsing had his own cage. Later, when they were more settled in, the two pandas would see, smell, and hear each other with a fence in between. Pandas in the wild and in captivity have been known to fight. The fence let Ling-Ling and Hsing-Hsing get used to each other's company before they would meet

Giant Panda presented from . .

提出從上大熊貓

The People's Republic of China

中國人民共和國

face-to-face in one enclosure. People hoped that Ling-Ling and Hsing-Hsing would become panda parents one day.

Both pandas were young when they arrived at the zoo. Ling-Ling was about eighteen months old and weighed 136 pounds. Hsing-Hsing was the same age, weighing just 74 pounds. The two pandas quickly put on weight, up to ten pounds a month. Fully grown giant pandas are four to six feet long and weigh more than two hundred pounds. Ling-Ling was a clown from the time she popped out of her crate. She lumbered around her pen, sniffed at a pot of bamboo, then took her water dish and put it on her head! Hsing-Hsing was much more cautious. He waited for five minutes after his crate was opened before coming out. He briefly looked around and then went into the small room that was his den. A special ceremony was held after Ling-Ling and Hsing-Hsing had settled in. First Lady Pat Nixon and other dignitaries from China and the United States welcomed the two pandas to America.

"Panda"-monium broke out after the eager public was invited to meet Ling-Ling and Hsing-Hsing.

Eight thousand people lined up for hours to see these two extraordinary pandas when they first went on display to the public.

Ling-Ling, the show-off of the pair, would do headstands and somersaults. She would jump up and down on her log pile. She would toss her ball. Sometimes, the pandas played, but more often than not, they ate and slept much as pandas do in the wild. Still, people were thrilled to see these two black-and-white ambassadors of goodwill. One visitor said, "They didn't do a lot, but [we liked] just to be able to look at them and know they

were so rare."
Three million
people came
each year to see
Ling-Ling and
Hsing-Hsing.
Ling-Ling and
Hsing-Hsing's arrival
signaled a new, more
friendly relationship
between Chinese and
American people. In addition
to the pandas' being symbols of
friendship, they are good for science.
Scientists hoped to study the growing
pandas in order to learn more about them.

Ling-Ling and Hsing-Hsing were a novelty for many people outside China. Giant pandas are naturally found only in the remote, cold, wet, mountainous Sichuan region of central China. The Chinese had known about giant pandas for centuries. But it wasn't until the French priest and naturalist Père David went to Sichuan to collect plants and animals that the western world first learned about these unique bears. Père David collected two panda bear skins, which he sent to Paris, France, in 1867 to be identified and studied. Before that time, no one outside of China knew about the existence of the shy, solitary wild pandas. Hidden in their mountainous home, the pandas ate the plentiful bamboo growing there (99 percent of their diet), roamed the forests, and raised their young, rarely encountering humans. For years, some people thought the pandas were related to raccoons. Others argued that the pandas were really bears. Today, thanks to pandas like Ling-Ling and Hsing-Hsing, we know pandas are members of the bear family. Since Ling-Ling and Hsing-Hsing came to the United States in 1972, much has been learned about these rare bears. Scientists have studied their diet and learned that, although bamboo is their favorite food, pandas will sometimes eat small animals. Scientists have studied how pandas breed in captivity, so more pandas can be raised. Pandas have also been studied more in the wild. There are only about sixteen hundred wild giant pandas left in China. These unique animals are now protected from hunters. Their forests are also protected from logging and agriculture.

In 1992, after being enjoyed by millions of zoo visitors, Ling-Ling died. She was twenty-three years old. Hsing-Hsing lived until 1999. Three giant pandas from China have taken the place of Ling-Ling and Hsing-Hsing. They live in a special enclosure that imitates their wild Chinese habitat. There is running water to drink and play in. There are shrubs, willows, and maples. There are fallen trees and rocks for Tai Shan, Mei Xiang, and Tian Tian to exercise on. They are given heavy-duty toys like plastic garbage cans and balls to play with. And of course, there is plenty of their favorite food, bamboo, growing in their enclosure.

Today, there are about three hundred pandas in zoos around the world. Most of these rare pandas are in Chinese zoos. But by working with other countries, China has ensured that millions of people will enjoy pandas far into the future.

Ling-Ling and Hsing-Hsing helped open the door for better friendship between China and the United States. These two pandas also opened the hearts of millions of Americans to help protect these unique animals.

Quest
(New York, New York)

On the morning of September 11, 2001, two planes crashed into the twin towers of the World Trade Center in New York City. A third plane crashed into the Pentagon in Washington DC. A fourth airplane crashed into a field outside Shanksville, Pennsylvania.

These events were the worst terrorist attacks in the history of the United States. Almost three thousand people died.

Hundreds of firefighters, police officers, and military personnel rushed to help victims of the attacks. Some of them died as they attempted to rescue survivors. As soon as they could, an estimated 350 search-and-rescue dogs, along with their handlers, arrived at the scenes of the three tragedies. The dogs' mission: to find anyone alive and then search for those who had died. These search-and-rescue dogs (SAR) came from all corners of the United States to help in this disaster. The terrorist attacks brought out the largest force of SAR dogs in United States history. Many dogs and their handlers have been singled out for their bravery and heroic efforts. These determined dogs spent days searching for victims of the attacks.

Quest (whose name means search) and his handler, Penny Sullivan, were just one of the many heroic search teams. Quest was a brown, black, and white German shepherd. Like all SAR dogs, Quest spent long hours training for just such a day as September 11, 2001. Quest and his companions were selected to be SAR dogs because they are intelligent, strong, and have remarkable endurance. They can search for hours before needing a rest. They possess superior senses of smell and hearing.

An SAR dog can smell at least one thousand times better than a human. They can hear things as far away as a quarter of mile.

SAR dogs are especially obedient, confident, and playful. Breeds with these characteristics include German shepherds, Labrador retrievers, Newfoundlands, golden retrievers, Belgian Malinois, and border collies. SAR dogs look for missing hikers.

They search for lost children. They crawl over avalanches, hoping to find anyone caught in the tumbling snow. They enter crumbled buildings. They risk their lives to help save humans in danger during floods, hurricanes, earthquakes, and other disasters.

SAR dogs undergo intense training to gain their unique skills. They learn to climb ladders, walk barefoot across broken glass, crawl under crumbled concrete ruins, wiggle into dark holes, and slip into small spaces, all while searching for the smell or sound of a human. The dogs are rewarded with lots of playing time and their favorite toys. And they get lots of love from their handlers and the families with whom they live.

Quest and Sullivan were called soon after the first plane hit the World Trade Center. Coming from nearby New Jersey, Sullivan said, "I remember driving down to Lakehurst [New Jersey] with my dog, Quest, and seeing the massive clouds of black smoke across the [Hudson] river." At Ground Zero, Quest and Sullivan waited in the smoke and dust until the command was given, "Bring the dogs!"

"The scene was incredible," Sullivan said. "Swirling smoke and dust and total destruction as far as the eye could see." She continued, "His [Quest's] body language was unmistakable. His interest was so intense. He would nose the area or gently paw at it with great concentration."

Sullivan rewarded Quest's heroic efforts with verbal praise. Unfortunately, Quest and Sullivan never got to play the rough game of tug-of-war they played as a celebration when Quest succeeded in finding someone alive.

For ten days, often working twelve to sixteen hours a day, Quest and Sullivan searched the hot, smoking, stinking ruins at Ground Zero. Sullivan said about Quest, "His attitude was excellent for the entire ten days." Sullivan said this about all of the SAR dog: "The dogs were absolutely amazing. All that work and training came into play. They moved over the twisted steel and debris with ease, even on beams stretching over burning pits below. It was clear the dogs were searching, as they had been trained, to find the missing victim hidden somewhere in the pile of rubble before them." At the end of each day's efforts, Sullivan and Quest went to a special station where veterinarians checked the dogs. Quest had a decontamination bath. His eyes, mouth, and ears were rinsed. His heart and lungs were checked. His paws were gently cleaned because he wore no protective pads. Quest went barefoot because he needed his claws for traction on the sloped surfaces of the collapsed buildings. Only after Quest was fed and given his bed did an exhausted Sullivan wash, eat, and sleep.

Besides searching for victims, Quest and many other SAR

dogs provided much-needed therapy for other workers at the disaster site. When not actively searching, Quest played with many weary human searchers. The much-saddened humans got comfort from petting Quest and whispering "thanks" to him. Sullivan said, "I think all of the dogs who served following 9/11 are true American heroes. They helped bring closure to countless families whose loved ones died in the attack[s]. But more importantly the dogs provided a sense of hope, a belief in the future, for their handlers, the workers and the families, and the nation as a whole."

On September 11, 2011, special ceremonies were held across the United States to remember the terrorist attacks in New York, Washington DC, and Pennsylvania. The dog heroes of 9/11 were honored across from Ground Zero at Liberty State Park in New Jersey. Finding One Another, a group established to "pay tribute to the rescue dogs who responded to Ground Zero," organized this special event. Hundreds of dogs and their handlers from across the country stood at attention as the 9/11 dogs still alive marched before them. The national anthem was played to honor these heroic dogs.

Unfortunately, Quest was not at the ceremony because he had died at age eleven in 2008. Sullivan was there, however, honoring Quest and all the SAR dogs that helped in so many ways after the 9/11 attacks.

Bucephalus

Cantor, Norman F. *Alexander the Great, Journey to the End of the Earth*. HarperCollins: New York, 2005.

Fox, Robin Lane. *The Search for Alexander*. Little, Brown: Boston, 1980.

Fox, Robin Lane. *Alexander the Great*. Penguin Books: New York, 2004.

Plutarch. *The Life of Alexander The Great*. The Modern Library: New York, 2004.

Seaman

Ambrose, Stephen. *Undaunted Courage*. Simon & Schuster, 1996.

Charbonneau, Louis. "Seaman's Trail: Fact vs. Fiction." *We Proceeded On*. November 1989 (pp. 6-12).

Osgood, Ernest S. "Our Dog Scannon." *Montana, The Magazine of Western History*. Summer 1976 (pp. 8-17).

Roop, Peter and Connie, eds. *Off the Map: The Journals of Lewis and Clark*. Walker, 1993.

National Park Service. nps.gov/archive/jeff/lewisclark/2/corpsofdiscovery

Old Abe

Zietlin, Richard. *Old Abe The War Eagle*. The State Historical Society of Wisconsin: Madison, WI, 1986.

"Old Abe, Fact and Fiction." *Badger History*, Volume 25 (November 1973).

"American Bald Eagle Information." BaldEagleInfo.com.

Punxsutawney Phil

Buchanan, Paul D. *Famous Animals of the States*. McFarland, 1996.

Community Information and Visitors Guide. "The Legend of Groundhog Day." Punxsutawney Chamber of Commerce pamphlet. 2011.

Hinterland Who's Who. "Woodchuck." http://www.hww.ca/hww2.asp?pid=1&id=109&cid=8. August 22, 2011.

Montgomery, Sy. "The Truth about Woodchucks." Animals .FindArticles.com. August 22, 2011. http://findarticles .com/p/articles/mi_m0FRO/is_5_133/ai_65539059/

Information from sign at Gobbler's Knob. May 2011.

Information at Punxsutawney, PA, library, outside Phil's burrow. May 2011.

Melina, Remy. "Life's Little Mysteries." January 2, 2011. www.lifeslittlemysteries.com/punxsutawney-phil-weather-prediction. September 20, 2011.

Woodchuck General Information. "Biology and Control of Woodchucks." http://pestproducts.com/woodchucks.htm.

Pelorus Jack

Alpers, Anthony. *Dolphins, the Myth and the Mammal*. Houghton Mifflin Company: Boston, 1961.

Interislander. www.interislander.co.nz. June 15, 2011.

"Pelorus Jack." *Encylopaedia of New Zealand*, 1966.

The Roosevelts' White House Pets

Driscoll, Laura. *Presidential Pets*. Grosset & Dunlap: New York, 2009.

Bishop, J.B., ed. *Theodore Roosevelt's Letters to His Children*. Scribner's: New York, 1919.

McCullough, John. *Mornings on Horseback*. Simon & Schuster: New York, 1981.

Rowan, Roy, and Brooke Janis. *First Dogs*. Algonquin: Chapel Hill, 2009.

Theodore Roosevelt Birthplace National Historic Site. "The Roosevelt Pets." Reprinted from the National Archives and Records Administration, Washington, DC.

The First Teddy Bear

Brinkley, Douglas. *The Wilderness Warrior*. HarperCollins: New York, 2009.

Bull, Peter. *The Teddy Bear Book*. Random House: New York, 1970.

Roop, Peter and Connie. *A Teddy Bear for President Roosevelt*. Scholastic: New York, 2002.

Smithsonian National Museum of American History. "Teddy Bear."

Teddy Bear and Friends. "The History of the Teddy Bear."

Mrs. Chippy

Alexander, Caroline. *Mrs. Chippy's Last Expedition*. Harper: New York, 1997.

Roop, Connie and Peter. *Escape From The Ice: Shackleton and the Endurance*. Scholastic: New York, 2001.

Worsley, F.A. *Endurance*. W.W. Norton: New York, 1931.

BBC News. "Antarctic hero 'reunited' with cat."

New Zealand Antarctic Society. "Mrs Chippy." www.antarctic.org.nz

"One of a Kind." *The New York Times*. November 21, 2004.

Balto

Buchanan, Paul D. *Famous Animals of the States.* McFarland & Co.: Jefferson, North Carolina, 1996.

George, Jean Craighead. *Incredible Animal Adventures.* Scholastic: New York, 1994.

Balto and the Hero Dogs of Alaska. Cleveland Museum of Natural History pamphlet. Cleveland, Ohio 44106.

Balto and the Legacy of the Serum Run. Cleveland Museum of Natural History pamphlet. Cleveland, Ohio 44106.

Standiford, Natalie. *The Bravest Dog Ever: The True Story of Balto.* Random House: New York, 1989.

www.baltotruestory.com. March 28, 2011.

Personal interviews with experts at Cleveland Museum of Natural History, Cleveland, Ohio 44106 in person, in May 2011, via phone in July 2011, and via e-mail in September.

Lonesome George

Facklam, Margery. *And Then There Was One.* Sierra Club Books: San Francisco, 1990.

Garcia Navarro, Lourdes. *Lonesome George, the Galápagos Giant Tortoise.* NPR. June 9, 2005.

Heller, Ruth. *Galápagos Means Tortoise.* Sierra Club Books for Children: San Francisco, 2000.

Nicholls, Henry. *Lonesome George: The Life and Loves of the World's Most Famous Tortoise.* Macmillan (Pan): 2006 (pp. 1, 55, 73, 67).

Seabiscuit

Beckwith, B.K. *Seabiscuit: The Saga of a Great Champion.* Westholme Publishing: Yardley, PA, 2003.

Dubowski, Kathy and Mark. *A Horse Named Seabiscuit.* Grosset & Dunlap: New York, 2003.

Hillenbrand, Laura. *Seabiscuit, An American Legend.* Ballantine Books: New York. 2001.

McEvoy, John, ed. *The Seabiscuit Story.* Eclipse Press: Lexington, Kentucky, 2003.

Shalton, Michelle. *The 10 Best Underdog Stories in Sports.* Scholastic: New York, 2008.

Smokey Bear

Barker, Elliot S. *Smokey Bear and the Great Wilderness.* Sunstone Press: Santa Fe, NM, 1982.

Forest History Society. Letter of Jul 8, 1950. United States Department of Agriculture Forest Service Press Release.

Koele, Catherine. "The Story of Smokey Bear." *Wisconsin DNR Wildfire Prevention Specialist.* *GLTPA Magazine,* March 2010 (pp. 38-40).

US Department of Agriculture. *The True Story of Smokey Bear.* Western Publishing, 1969.

Nelson, Steve, and Jack Rollins. "Smokey the Bear." US Department of Agriculture. Hill & Range Songs, 1952.

US Department of Agriculture. "Smokey's Story." SmokeyBear.com.

Andre

Goodridge, Harry, and Lew Dietz. *A Seal Called Andre: The Two Worlds of a Maine Harbor Seal.* Down East Books: Camden, Maine, 1975.

"Pose for the camera, Andre." p. 75.

Hodgkins, Fran. Andre: *The Famous Harbor Seal.* Down East Books: Camden, Maine, 2003.

Koko

Patterson, Francine. *The Education of Koko.* Holt, Rinehart & Winston: New York, 1981

Patterson, Francine. *Koko's Story.* Scholastic: New York, 1987.

Patterson, Francine. *Koko's Kitten.* DVD.

The Gorilla Foundation. www.KoKo.org. 2009.

A Conversation with Koko. Nature DVD. Questar, Inc.: Chicago, 2004.

Ling-Ling and Hsing-Hsing

Collins, Larry, and James Page. *Ling-Ling and Hsing-Hsing, Year of the Panda.* Anchor Press: New York, 1973.

Nicholls, Henry. *The Way of the Panda.* Pegasus Books: New York, 2011.

Smithsonian National Zoological Park. "Giant Panda."

"Ling-Ling Dies Suddenly." *The Washington Post.* December 31, 1992.

Quest

Bauer, Nona Kilgore. *Dog Heroes of September 11th.* Kennel Club Books: Allenhurst, NJ, 2006.

"March to Honor Rescue Dogs From 9/11." *Pittsburgh Post-Gazette.* September 10, 2011.

"Rescue Dogs of 9/11: The Drama's Unsung Heroes." *New York Post.* September 4, 2011.

"9/11 Rescue Dogs Honored at Liberty State Park Ceremony." NJ.com. September 11, 2011.

Suffolk County SPCA. "The Suffolk County SPCA at Ground Zero."